THE FLIPPED LEARNING SERIES

flipped learning
for
Science
INSTRUCTION

JONATHAN BERGMANN
AARON SAMS

T0131276

International Society for Technology in Education
EUGENE, OREGON • ARLINGTON, VA

The Flipped Learning Series
Flipped Learning for Science Instruction
Jonathan Bergmann and Aaron Sams

Editor: *Paul Wurster*
Associate Editor: *Emily Reed*
Production Manager: *Lynda Gansel*
Copy Editor: *Kristin Landon*
Proofreader: *Ann Skaugset*
Book Interior Design and Production: *Kim McGovern*

First Edition
ISBN: 978-1-56484-359-3 (paperback)
ISBN: 978-1-56484-500-9 (e-book)

Printed in the United States of America

About ISTE

The International Society for Technology in Education (ISTE) is the premier nonprofit organization serving educators and education leaders committed to empowering connected learners in a connected world. ISTE serves more than 100,000 education stakeholders throughout the world.

ISTE's innovative offerings include the ISTE Conference & Expo, one of the biggest, most comprehensive ed tech events in the world—as well as the widely adopted ISTE Standards for learning, teaching and leading in the digital age and a robust suite of professional learning resources, including webinars, online courses, consulting services for schools and districts, books, and peer-reviewed journals and publications. Visit iste.org to learn more.

Also by Jonathan Bergmann and Aaron Sams

Flipped Learning: Gateway to Student Engagement

Flip Your Classroom: Reach Every Student in Every Class Every Day

Flip Your Classroom—The Workbook: Making Flipped Learning Work for You

About the Authors

Jon Bergmann is a teacher who used to love being the center of the classroom. But he gave it up when he saw how engaged his students became in the learning process when he began flipping his instruction. Flipped learning allowed him to know his students better which brought him back to the reason he became a teacher in the first place. He is considered one of the pioneers of flipped learning and now shares his passion for learner-centered classrooms with educators around the globe. Jon is currently chief learning officer of FlippedClass.com. He received the Presidential Award for Excellence in Math and Science Teaching in 2002 and was named a semi-finalist for Colorado Teacher of the Year in 2010. Jon serves on the advisory board of TED Education and hosts "The Flip Side," a radio show which tells the stories of flipped educators. Additionally, he is a founding board member and the treasurer of the Flipped Learning Network, the only not-for-profit organization run by and for flipped educators.

Aaron Sams has been an educator since 2000. He is managing director of FlippedClass.com, co-founder of The Flipped Learning Network, and is an adjunct professor at Saint Vincent College. He was awarded the 2009 Presidential Award for Excellence in Math and Science Teaching and was a chemistry teacher in Woodland Park, CO, and in Hacienda Heights, CA. Aaron also served as co-chair of the Colorado State Science Standards Revision Committee and serves as an advisor to TED-Ed. Aaron co-authored *Flip Your Classroom: Reach Every Student in Every Class Every Day* and *Flipped Learning: Gateway to Student Engagement.* He frequently speaks and conducts workshops on educational uses of screencasts and the flipped classroom concept. He advocates for inquiry-based and student-centered learning environments in which students are encouraged to demonstrate their understanding in ways that are meaningful to them. With experience in public, private, and home schools, in face-to-face, online, and blended learning environments, Aaron brings a unique educational perspective to any audience. He is a lifelong learner, reader, maker, and explorer. He holds a BS in Biochemistry and an MAEd, both from Biola University.

Contents

Contents

Preface

As the first days of school began in 2006, we—Aaron Sams and Jonathan Bergmann—arrived to teach science at Woodland Park High School in Woodland Park, Colorado. Jon came from the Denver metropolitan area and settled into room 313, and Aaron came from the greater Los Angeles area to occupy room 314.

We had both taught chemistry at our previous schools, Jon for 18 years and Aaron for 6 years. Because we represented the entire chemistry team, we decided to work together to develop a strong chemistry program at Woodland Park.

During the school year, we taught traditionally, using a great deal of direct instruction in an engaging lecture style. We also met on a regular basis to reflect about best practices and how to integrate technology into our classes. These voluntary meetings grew out of the fact that we worked together well and realized that two heads were better than one.

In the spring of 2007, Aaron showed Jon an article that reviewed a computer program that recorded PowerPoint lectures, including digital ink that could be written on the screen and audio recording. At this point, we were ready to dive into the world of teacher-created video.

We first used screen-recording software to capture live lectures. Once we started, the assistant superintendent in charge of curriculum and instruction in our school district took note and visited our classrooms. Her daughter was attending university, and one of her daughter's professors was recording the audio of his lectures. She told us that her daughter loved this model because she didn't have to go to class anymore. Later that week during lunch, a conversation about that interaction ensued. What is the value of class time if a student can access all the content while not attending class? What do students *really* need a teacher physically present for?

In that conversation Aaron asked Jon, "What if we stopped lecturing in class and pre-recorded all of our lessons, and in class students could do the stuff that they used to do at home?" Jon said, "OK, lets do it!" Since then, neither of us has used direct instruction as a whole-group, in-class teaching method.

During this time of development, we shared what we were doing with a group of teachers online. These teachers had been active on the AP Chemistry listserv for many years and used that platform to connect and learn from other AP Chemistry teachers from around the world. This group became a place to share and learn, as well as a sounding board, as the concept of the flipped classroom grew. The flipped classroom was not born in a vacuum. It did not develop in rooms 313 and 314 alone. There are now many communities of practice around the world for teachers who are implementing the flipped class. We, along with Dr. Jerry Overmeyer at the University of Northern Colorado, oversee one community at flippedclassroom.org that has more than 25,000 members. Though we get much of the credit for the flipped classroom, it would never have happened without the broader network of other amazing teachers.

The idea of the flipped classroom is really quite simple. Direct instruction is done through video, or some other digital learning object, which students can use individually before they come to class. This time shift allows the teacher to use class time for work that either is better done as a large group or requires individualized attention by the teacher. That's it. The flipped class, in brief, is direct instruction delivered to the individual outside of class, so there is more strategic use of in-class time for group work and individualized attention. We soon found out that we had stumbled on something that could radically transform our classrooms into something we never could have anticipated.

We have chronicled much of this in our previous books, *Flip Your Classroom: Reach Every Student in Every Class Every Day* (Bergmann & Sams, 2012), and *Flipped Learning: Gateway to Student Engagement* (Bergmann & Sams, 2014). Since the publication of those two books, teachers have been asking us for very specific resources on how to flip different subjects and grade levels. This book is part of a series of books designed to meet that demand.

This book is a practical guide for science teachers interested in flipping their classrooms. It helps science teachers deal with the realities of teaching in an increasingly interconnected and digital world. This book serves as a guide for science teachers who are beginning to flip their classes or who are interested in exploring the flipped model for the first time. Each chapter explores practical ways to bring flipped learning into the science classroom, including:

- How to flip your class and the four hurdles to flipping (thinking, technology, time, and training).

- How your approach to planning changes as you implement flipped learning.

- How flipping will enhance the science laboratory experience for students.

- How you can use traditional resources such as textbooks and the internet.

- What to do in class once you have flipped your class.

- How to implement the flipped-mastery model into a science classroom.

- How flipped learning can work alongside learning through scientific inquiry.

- How flipped learning can provide an environment where projects can be done more often and with more fidelity.

We begin with a story about one of our students that illustrates how flipped learning can enhance achievement and really change a person's life.

Chapter 1

why you should flip your class

FLIPPED LEARNING has a deep impact on the professional lives of teachers, but more important, flipped learning positively affects the lives of students. The following is a true story about one of our former students.

Alyssa was a bright and energetic young person who didn't perform particularly well in school. She was her own person. She would frequently change her hair color to match her mood. Alyssa was a free spirit and a bit awkward. She didn't fit the mold as a typical student either socially or academically. She had not earned great grades. They were not bad, but they were not great. Alyssa was extremely bright, but she was not a student who played the game of school very well. School didn't seem relevant to her, and she often wondered why she was there. To some degree, she resented her teachers for constantly pressing her to simply get things done. Ultimately, she wanted more control of her learning. However, her lack of effort had taken its toll. Because she resented school, she had missed some key points in her learning and had some significant gaps. Her math background was weak, and she was a little bit behind other students with similar academic abilities.

We have all had students like Alyssa who don't like to play the game that school often is, and other students who are behind for a variety of other reasons. How can we reach students like Alyssa, provide for their needs, and create a place where the Alyssas of the world will engage and fulfill their potential?

Alyssa was one of the first students to learn in Jon's flipped-mastery chemistry course. She stepped into a world where she had more control of her learning, could get the extra support she needed to help with her deficiencies, and could create better relationships and connections with her peers and her teacher. That first year Alyssa realized that she did not have to simply sit and listen to Jon. She could actively engage him in conversation one-on-one, get help in areas she struggled in, and discover a passion for science she never knew she had.

Toward the end of the year, she asked Jon if she should take Advanced Placement (AP) Chemistry. Jon, knowing that AP Chemistry would be a huge stretch for her, encouraged her to do it. Because AP Chemistry was also a flipped course, he realized she would have more support to help her. The following year she was in Aaron's AP Chemistry course, and it was in that class that Alyssa came into her own as a learner and as a scientist. She realized she had what it took to be something great. Her mother approached Jon and thanked us for creating a spark in her daughter that gave her courage to succeed in something she would have never thought possible. Because Alyssa had started high school behind, she really struggled with AP Chemistry. That summer she got her score, and she had earned a 1 out of a possible 5. Not very good, but something had awakened in Alyssa.

During her senior year, she approached Aaron to ask if she could continue to work in chemistry. She did a senior independent research project where she created a fuel cell powered by the sun that charged a mobile device. Through this project, she learned a great deal of the material she hadn't learned during her previous two years in chemistry.

The story gets better. Alyssa applied and was accepted to the Colorado School of Mines and ended up pursuing a degree in mining engineering, graduating in the spring of 2015. Alyssa attributes much of her success to learning in a flipped classroom, and the greatest share of that success she attributes to the relationships she established with teachers and the support they provided on her journey from struggling student to engineer. Our hope is that this book will help science teachers reach students like Alyssa who need more autonomy and more control over their learning. We also hope this book will help science teachers reach not only students like Alyssa, but all of their students, by awakening each of them to the possibilities that lie ahead.

Flipped Class 101

Simplicity is the ultimate sophistication.

—LEONARDO DA VINCI

Sometimes the simplest ideas are the most profound. Think back to BlackBerry phones with their many buttons. Everybody wanted one—until Steve Jobs of

Apple told his design team to create a phone with *one* button. And, as they say, the rest is history. The flipped class technique at its core is a simple idea, based on these two steps:

- Move the direct instruction (often called the lecture) away from the group space. This usually means that students watch and interact with an instructional video (flipped video) before coming to class.

- Repurpose class time that you freed up from direct instruction and use it to practice learned concepts, engaging activities, and higher order thinking.

We call this simple time-shift Flipped Class 101, and this reflects what people popularly refer to as a flipped classroom. Flip the homework with the direct instruction, and you have a flipped class. This simple time shift has significant benefits, such as the following:

- In a typical classroom, students often go home with difficult homework. They do this work independently and have little or no help. Some are successful, but many are not. In a flipped class, students do the difficult tasks in class with an expert present, the teacher.

- Because the presentation of content is removed from class time, there is more time for teachers to interact and help students.

- Students can pause and rewind a video. In a typical class, you cannot pause your teacher.

There are many other benefits, which we have chronicled in our previous books, mentioned earlier. The focus of this book is to give science teachers practical strategies to help them reach students using the flipped model.

The One Question

Another way to think about the simplicity of the flipped classroom model is to boil it down to one simple question: *What is the best use of your face-to-face class time?* Is the best use of the valuable time with students content dissemination of information, or is it something else? In a flipped classroom setting, the direct instruction is offloaded to the individual space, and the class time is used for something else. In science classes, this "something else" is more hands-on lab time, more inquiry, more projects, and more guided practice time with the teacher present.

We began pioneering this instructional model in 2006 for our Chemistry, AP Chemistry, and Earth & Space classes. At first, our simplistic answer to the question about best use of face-to-face time was that we wanted our students to have more time to get help on their assignments from us and for our students to conduct more experiments. When we flipped our science classes, our students performed significantly better on our unit exams, and we were able to do 50% more labs (Bergmann & Sams, 2014). What started as an experiment to help meet the needs of our students became a new technique that radically changed our classrooms and the classrooms of many other teachers.

Given that we experienced success with this model, you would expect that we would continue to use it. However, after the first year of the flipped class, we didn't simply repeat the previous year; we reinvented our class again and added mastery learning to our repertoire. Based on the work of Benjamin Bloom (1968), the flipped-mastery model is an asynchronous approach in which students demonstrate mastery of content before moving to new topics. Each student moves at a flexible pace, which allows advanced students to get the challenges they need and provides extra support for students who struggle. The next year we began to bring in more inquiry, especially using Process Oriented Guided Inquiry Learning

(POGIL, http://pogil.org). The point is that we kept iterating and changing to improve our class and move beyond the flipped classroom.

Beyond the Flipped Class

Why do we call it Flipped Class 101? Though we believe the flipped class is a viable method with benefits over more traditional forms of instruction, we feel you can take the flipped class to the next level. We see teachers flip their classrooms for one to two years and then move to deeper learning strategies such as flipped-mastery, or a more inquiry- or project-based model. These we categorize not as flipped classrooms, but as flipped learning. Flipped learning is the second iteration of the flipped classroom where teachers move beyond the basic Flipped Class 101 model to more content-rich, inquiry-driven, project-based classes. We chronicle this transformation thoroughly in our book *Flipped Learning: Gateway to Student Engagement*. We will share how these strategies work specifically in a science class toward the end of this book.

Chapter 2

flipped class
101

THOUGH THE FLIPPED CLASSROOM model is a simple idea, it can be complex for teachers to implement. Simply telling students to watch a video and then come to class to learn more deeply sounds good, but what if students do not watch the video? What if students do not have access to technology at home? What is a teacher to do then?

There are four major hurdles to flipping that you need to overcome. These are:

- Flipping your thinking

- Technological barriers

- Finding the time

- Training yourself, students, and parents

Flipping Your Thinking

Flipping your thinking as a science teacher may be the *most* important hurdle to overcome. Why is this a big hurdle? Perhaps it is because many of us have been "doing school" the same way for many years and find change to be difficult.

Jon spent 19 years as a lecture/discussion teacher. He knew how to teach that way very well. In fact, he reached the point where if you told him the topic of the day, he could probably start teaching that topic without any notes simply from his years of experience. In 2007, when we decided to begin using video as our primary means of direct instruction, Jon was the hesitant one. He didn't want to give up lecture time. He was a good lecturer (or at least he thought he was). He liked being the center of attention and enjoyed engaging a whole group of students in science instruction. His class was well structured, and he liked being in control of all that was happening. So, when he flipped his class, he had to surrender control of the learning to the students. That was not easy, but it was the best thing he ever did in his teaching career.

Anyone born before the 1990s grew up in an information-scarce world in which we had to search through card catalogs and microfiche to access information. Information was localized at the schoolhouses, in the libraries, in textbooks, and in the heads of our teachers. Today, students can access virtually any information by simply using a device they most likely have in their pocket.

In light of this change, we must rethink how we teach our students. Think of any topic you currently teach— for example, the Big Bang Theory, the theory of plate tectonics, photosynthesis, or oxidation–reduction reactions. A quick search of YouTube reveals myriad videos available explaining these concepts. So the bigger question is this: How do we teach when our students have an oversupply of information?

Technological Barriers of the Flipped Classroom

Many educators have pigeonholed the flipped class model as a technological solution to education. Much of the buzz about flipping has to do with using video as an instructional tool, and that does involve a technological component. However, we disagree with those who see flipped learning as a technology-based educational practice. We see it as a pedagogical solution with an underlying technological component.

What, then, are the technological tools you need to master to flip your science class?

Teachers often ask us this question: "What is the best tool to flip my class?" To which we respond, "It is the one you will *actually* use." Our answer to this question has a lot to do with you and your skills and needs. What type of a computer do you have? Do you have tablets? Do your students have devices? What is your comfort level with technology?

There is a whole host of available technology tools. Some are very easy to use and are limited in features, whereas others are more complicated, offering more powerful features that add to the production values of your content. We understand that not all teachers are tech experts, so the tool you might use has a high degree of variability. We do see a few categories of technological tools that teachers must master to flip a class effectively. Before we discuss them, we should address a key question.

Who Should Make the Videos?

Should you make the flipped videos when there are videos on every conceivable science topic already on YouTube? There is no question that anything you teach has probably been posted, but we believe that one of the hallmarks of a successful flipped classroom is the use of videos created by the teacher or a team of teachers at the local school. When we visit *struggling* flipped classrooms, we often see that the teacher is simply assigning video content created either commercially or by teachers outside their immediate network rather than making their own. Conversely, when we walk into *successful* flipped classrooms, we usually find that the teacher is the video creator. We think the reason teacher-created videos are more successful is because they involve one of the fundamental features of good teaching: relationships with kids who know you! You are their teacher. Some random person on the internet is *not* as familiar. Students see your investment in them through the content you provide. They recognize that someone who has direct involvement in their lives created custom content for them.

Video Creation Tools

As of the writing of this book (bearing in mind that technology tools are always in flux), we continually observe five categories of video creation tools teachers are using to create flipped class videos: video cameras, document cameras, screencasting programs, tablet apps, and smart pens.

Video cameras. The easiest tool for most teachers to use is the camera built into their phone. Virtually all modern mobile phones have a video camera built in, and inexpensive handheld video cameras are capable of producing very high quality video. A teacher could have someone (a colleague or student) use a camera or phone to record the teacher teaching a concept at a chalkboard. This is ideal for things like balancing chemical equations, solving a motion problem, or doing Punnett squares. This method would not be as good for topics where you would need extensive pictures, such as discussing Pangaea or the location of the ulna in an anatomy class.

Document cameras. Many teachers have also used their document cameras to make flipped class videos. Many don't realize that this camera, which is designed to project an image in real time, can also record. When the document camera is hooked up to a computer (typically through a USB port), the software that came with the document camera often has the ability to record the screen. Therefore, whatever a teacher does under the document camera can be recorded along with the teacher's voice. For example, a teacher describing an igneous rock can be pointing to the different crystals. Then they can switch to paper notes. All of this can be converted into a video that can be shared with students.

Screencasting programs. These programs record whatever is happening on your computer screen along with the audio, and in some cases, even a webcam shot. Screencasting is the number-one choice for flipped class teachers to make videos. Typically, they create a lesson or presentation in some sort of presentation software such as Microsoft PowerPoint and use a screencasting program to record them teaching through their slide deck. There are even ways for the teacher to digitally write on the presentation so the students see the presentation, hear the teacher's voice, see a webcam of the teacher in the corner, and see whatever the teacher writes on the screen.

Tablet apps. Many apps for tablet devices can be used to make video recordings. Some popular apps include:

- Knowmia (www.knowmia.com)

- Explain Everything (www.morriscooke.com)

- Doceri (http://doceri.com)

- Educreations (www.educreations.com)

One advantage of tablet devices is that it is easy to write on the presentation. For many of these you can upload a presentation to the tablet and then record the presentation. The tablet interface is an ideal choice when you need to annotate over pictures or want to have typical chalkboard features.

Smart pens. A variety of smart pens are available that will digitally record what is written on paper as well as the user's voice. The recordings are then converted into video files (often called pencasts), which can be shared online. Some of these pens require the use of special paper that can be purchased or printed.

Hosting Videos

Once you finish creating a video, you have to upload it to the internet for students to access. A large number of video hosting sites are available. The easiest, and most familiar, to use is YouTube, assuming your school district does not block the site. YouTube is good in that the vast majority of students know how to access it, and if they have a device, it most certainly plays YouTube videos.

But if you don't want to or cannot post videos to YouTube, videos can be placed on other video hosting sites such as Vimeo, TeacherTube, or Screencast.com. You can also post videos to the school website or to a learning management system (LMS).

Making Videos Interactive

Once a flipped video is created and posted online, it is important to not just tell students to watch the video. Simply watching a video is a passive activity for students. Students are familiar with watching Hollywood movies where they passively view something designed to entertain. Watching an instructional video, where students must come away with some level of understanding, is a very different activity. We recommend that teachers build interactivity into the videos. There is no single way to do this. You could have students simply take notes on the video, or have them respond to an online forum, or use some other creative strategy. There are even software and web tools available that pause a video at specified times, causing a teacher-generated question to pop up. The teacher then has access to user logs to identify who watched the video, and how each student responded to the questions. Regardless of which tool is used, the key is to make sure students are actively engaged with the content and have something to do as they watch.

Making Flipped Videos Easy to Access

It is important to find an easy way to post video content, but it is equally (and maybe more) important to make it easy for students to access the videos. Learning management systems are a category of websites that allow a teacher or entire school to organize digital content in one place. Students log in and interact with digital content in some fashion. An LMS can host videos, store online documents for students to view, and have forums, blogs, and quizzing and assessment features. This software can be one-stop shopping for students to access all materials needed for a particular class. Examples of learning management systems include Moodle,

Blackboard, Canvas, Schoology, Edmodo, Haiku Learning, My Big Campus, and a number of others. Each of them has advantages and disadvantages. Our recommendation is that schools adopt one system as an institution so that students get all of their digital content from one site.

Instead of using an LMS, some teachers have simply printed up a short notes sheet with a quick response (QR) code on the top. Scanning the QR code with a smartphone app leads students to the video, and they take notes directly on the paper handout. These teachers are not using an LMS but are simply hosting their videos on the internet; students access them directly from the printed notes sheet.

One thing we have been noticing lately is a new breed of LMS that is adding gamification. Instead of students going to a site to access content and interact with it, there is a gaming component where students can unlock conditionally released options and quests. Once students have completed a quest, they can earn experience points or badges. Teachers are using these points and badges as an alternate way to report progress because it connects with students in a familiar way.

I Want Specific Tools

Writing a book that recommends specific tech tools is difficult because technology changes so quickly. If you are in search of just the right tool for you, we have created and placed a series of videos on our website that feature several tools for video creation, hosting, and all things technological for the flipped classroom. You can find these videos at http://FlippedClass.com/tools. You can also scan the QR code in Figure 2.1 to reach this website.

FIGURE 2.1 A quick response code that leads to http://FlippedClass.com/tools.

Finding the Time

Time is an elusive commodity. Where can you find the time to create all these videos, post them on a website, build in interactivity, and recreate your classroom activities? We wish we had a magic answer to tell you how to find the time, but we don't. To be honest, successful flipped class teachers just make the time, and even more successful flipped teachers collaborate and work together to maximize their time. Flipping your class will not make teaching easier, but it will make it better. We carved out time before or after school where we committed to making this happen. We were seeing such positive results that we felt we had to do this for our students, and the work necessary to accomplish this task was worth it to us.

If your school or district leadership is supportive of the flipped classroom model, there are things they can do to provide you the time you will need to get started. The following are suggestions you and your school leadership might discuss:

- Hire substitute teachers for a day, and have two teachers plan and create videos and in-class activities.

- Use Professional Learning Team time to create shared video assets and other learning objects.

- Schedule common planning time for teachers.

- Use staff professional learning time to focus on flipping the class.

Training Yourself, Students, and Parents

The last hurdle to flipping a class is for all involved in flipping to get the appropriate training to implement the model well. There are two primary aspects of training to address.

Teach Students How to Watch Videos

Assigning videos and assuming students will watch them is a common mistake teachers make. Students need to know *how* to watch an instructional video. We have discovered that this is not something that will come naturally to students. They need specific instructions on how to *interact* with the videos. We suggest you watch the first few videos in class with your students while modeling how you want your students to interact.

Pause the video frequently and discuss how they should be listening, viewing, and thinking about the subject matter. Then have students watch the next video individually in class while you supervise and ensure they are appropriately learning from the video. Keep in mind that not all students will master all the content by simply viewing a video. The point of the video is to introduce content so that students can master the content *in class* with the real expert present—the teacher. We did this for an entire week with our high school chemistry students, but we have heard from middle school teachers who take as much as three weeks to teach students how to interact with video content.

Get the Training You Need

Learning how to flip a science class is not just about assigning a video and doing more labs in class. It is so much more. You must plan, engage, develop, and revise. Find what works best for you in your setting and take what works. We like to say there is not one way to flip a class. Each flipped classroom looks different, and it should.

Some teachers have assigned a video as homework and discovered that students didn't watch it—and have given up on the flipped class. Setting up a successful flipped class requires thought and planning. The best way to set yourself up for success is to network with other teachers who flip their class, attend a training session or conference on flipping your class, and ask many questions. Teachers need to consider many things before they jump into a flipped class model.

In the next chapter, we address key considerations for the flipped science classroom, such as planning lessons, keeping students engaged, and managing the chaos.

Chapter 3

planning
for the
flipped classroom

WE ALL LEARNED how to plan a lesson, a unit, or a year in our education courses in college. Many of the models for planning lessons are effective, but when the flipped classroom model is in place, several of these frameworks need to be re-addressed. Most planning structures (and the teacher evaluation instruments) imply, or even explicitly state, that there will be some sort of upfront presentation of information to the whole class. In a fully flipped classroom, the direct instruction is at the individual level or in small groups. This means that planning a flipped lesson requires modifying its planning and delivery cycle. The easiest adaptation is to make a time-shift in the lesson. Shift the direct instruction out of the class space, and the independent practice back into the class space. Complex rearrangements of lesson elements are certainly possible in a flipped class. A simple shift in time and space allows a teacher to implement the flipped model even if they are working in an environment that does not allow much flexibility in lesson planning. In the following sections, we will break this down by looking at how to organize a unit, a week, and a day.

Flipping a Unit

How does planning a unit change when you implement a flipped model? In many ways, there is no great need to change how you plan a unit. Figure 3.1 is a chart of a unit we used in our chemistry course. We identified each of our learning objectives, tied this with practice and hands-on activities, and created a video. Our assumption is that most science teachers already have a list of objectives similar to this chart. They have some practice activities (we created worksheets) and some hands-on experiments. Most likely, these are in place in most classes, with the exception of the creation of a video. Therefore, the only new thing a teacher needs to do is create a flipped video.

	Objective	Learning Objects	Required Activities
Gases-1	Be able to understand how gases differ from solids and liquids and how gas pressure is measured.	Video 1 Worksheet 1 Text Section 12.1–12.2	
Gases-2	Be able to conceptually and mathematically explain Boyle's Law, Charles's Law, and Gay-Lussac's Law.	Video 2 Worksheet 2 Text Section 12.3	Online Simulation Boyle's Law Lab Charles's Law Lab
Gases-3	Be able to calculate using the Combined Gas Law.	Video 3 Worksheet 3 Text Section 12.3	Take Home Lab
Gases-4	Be able to calculate using the Ideal Gas Law.	Video 4 Worksheet 4 Text Section 12.4	
Gases-5	Be able to conceptually and mathematically explain Dalton's Law of Partial Pressure and Graham's Law of Diffusion.	Video 5 Worksheet 5 Text Section 12.5	Graham's Law Demo
Gases-6	Be able to do gas-stoichiometry where gases are not collected at standard temperature and pressure.	Video 6 Worksheet 6 Text Section 12.5	Gas Stoichiometry Lab
Gases-7	Be able to determine the molar mass of a gas that is collected at non-standard conditions.	Video 7 Worksheet 7 Text Section: Not in Text	

FIGURE 3.1 One of our charts for a chemistry unit on gases.

One benefit of taking this approach is that it presses us as teachers to be very organized with content. The process of writing down objectives and creating or curating appropriate learning objects is a powerful process that teachers should implement regardless of whether they flip. Figure 3.1 is an example of such an organizing document. This kind of careful planning helps teachers to be thoughtful about which resources and assessments best fit each objective. This process is also helpful to those who often fly a bit by the seats of their pants—us included! Before we flipped our classes, we often walked in and "taught" what we wanted or just explained what was next in the curriculum. When

Chapter 3 · Planning for the Flipped Classroom

we got serious about the flipped classroom, we realized we had to be much more organized about how we were teaching science. This single exercise dramatically helped us to think through what was taught, how it was taught, and what things we should stop teaching.

Flipping a Week

Once a teacher plans a unit, how do they plan for a week? In many ways, a teacher's planning cycle does not need to change too dramatically. If a teacher has a flipped video they have created or curated, they need to build in a few extra steps to ensure that students don't just watch the video, but also interact with it. Here are a couple suggestions for how to modify a typical weekly planning guide with the flip in mind:

- Give extra time and/or advance notice. Don't assign a video for one night and expect all students to complete the homework. Students may need more advance notice. Some students are overprogrammed and are on the go from the moment school ends. Trying to get some time in front of an internet-connected device at the last minute may be a challenge for such students.

- Allow some choice. Not every student needs to watch every video. The key is not that they *watched* something, but rather that they *learned* something. For example, if there is an online simulation that teaches the principles of plate tectonics, have students interact with that *instead* of watching a video.

Flipping a Day

Flipping a day in isolation (as a teaching strategy) can often be more difficult than flipping a whole unit or a class. This is because students are often not "trained" in learning in a flipped classroom setting. However, many teachers' first entry point in the flipped classroom is to flip a few lessons. They may only use a flipped lesson once every week or two. The key to flipping a day is to have the lower level cognitive content presented on video and have an engaging activity during class time.

Keeping Students Engaged

When Jon first started to flip his Earth & Space science course, he wanted to have many hands-on activities for his students to engage with during the class time. At first, he had students doing experiments and activities almost every day. He soon realized that he was doing too many labs. The pace for his students was too frantic, and they got to the point where they were just trying to get through the labs instead of really learning from them. What his students needed was more time to simply work on assigned class problems and exercises. He realized students needed to practice and process their learning individually with his help.

We have also seen the other extreme where teachers have students watch a video at home, complete worksheets in class, but aren't offered any hands-on activities. This repeats day after day. Though students need time to process and practice, they also need engaging activities with which to interact. If the only change you make is flipping the time of day you deliver direct instruction and have students complete worksheets, you have not made pedagogical changes; you have merely made temporal changes.

There are two ends of the spectrum where a teacher can err, and landing on either end of the spectrum can lead to disengaged students (see Figure 3.2). Try to find a balance, a "sweet spot," where students have time for engaging hands-on activities *and* time to process content with you, the expert teacher, present.

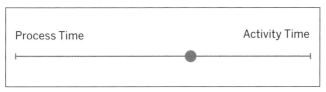

FIGURE 3.2 Finding the balance, or "sweet spot," between time for processing content and activity time maximizes student engagement.

Managing the Chaos

One of the biggest struggles flipped class teachers face is choosing which students to help when. Because teachers are constantly moving around the room assisting students, what often happens is that the students who are the most demanding get the help and attention. And, as you know, the most demanding students are not always the ones who need the most help. In a flipped class, we need to be cognizant of which students need more help, which ones are ready for the next challenge, and which ones have learned something incorrectly and need clarification. There are no easy ways to determine which students need the most assistance. That changes from day to day and even moment to moment. Frankly, this is part of the art of teaching and the dance of the classroom that is difficult to quantify, but it must be managed.

We had students come find us when they needed help, but this resulted in too many students standing in line and waiting for help. This also affected how willing students were to find us. One strategy you might try to identify students in need is to employ a visual cue. Cara Johnson, an anatomy teacher in Texas, uses a set of three colored plastic cups at each table to create a quick visual trigger identifying which students need help. A green cup indicates that students are fine and do not need any help; a yellow cup indicates that the group has a question but does not need an immediate answer; and a red cup indicates that the table of students are at an impasse and need immediate assistance. Using a system such as the cups helps students subtly indicate to their teacher their level of need, and it gives a teacher a way to assess individual and group needs quickly.

In the next chapter, we will explore how to enhance labs and hands-on activities in a flipped science classroom.

Chapter 4

flipping the lab

HOW MANY TIMES have you asked students to do a pre-lab, and then on the day of the actual lab, had to spend most of the class time going over everything you wanted them to learn in the pre-lab? Have you been frustrated with your limited class time and wished your students had more time to conduct a lab experiment? Enter "Flipping the Lab."

As science teachers, we know students never have enough time to finish their labs. Many science teachers have shortened class times, and this makes it difficult to fit in lab instructions, lab investigations, and then lab analysis in a typical class period. One way to deal with the time problem is to flip the pre-lab by creating a short video, which prepares students to start the experiment with little or no in-class direction from the teacher. To accomplish this, students watch a demonstration of the steps they will conduct during the experiment, and then conduct the experiment in class.

Flipping Lab Techniques

One way to get more out of lab time is to have students watch videos about lab techniques beforehand. These videos are great for introducing students to some typical science practices, such as how to titrate, how to test the hardness of a rock, or how to use a scale. Note that many students will not have mastered techniques by just interacting with a video. This will simply be a way to introduce them to the technique with the intent that the students will develop the skill while using it in the lab. And, by using flipped videos to learn lab techniques, students will have more time in class to master the specific skill.

We created a video for teaching students how to use a volumetric pipet bulb. This skill is difficult for students to master, and it simply takes time. Having students watch it ahead of time allowed for more time in class to practice the skill. At first we had them practicing with water, and then eventually had them pipet chemicals for a variety of experiments. Using the instructional video gave students some basic background before attempting this difficult skill.

Flipping Lab Safety

A good entry point to the flipped science classroom is to flip lab safety instruction at the beginning of the year. Jennifer Maze, a chemistry teacher in Colorado, starts the school year with a video showing her making several poor decisions in the lab. This humorous video illustrates to students not only the importance of lab safety, but also how to conduct oneself properly in the lab. Maze then follows this up with a typical lab safety quiz, which ensures that students truly understand the unique nature of safety in the science lab. An added benefit of flipping lab safety is that students who enroll in the class at any time after the beginning of the year can receive the same safety message as students who started the year in class.

FIGURE 4.1 Chemistry teacher Jennifer Maze (right) and her colleagues at Falcon High School demonstrate lab safety in a pre-lab video.

Student-Created Pre-Lab Videos

Another thing Maze does is to have students create pre-lab videos for other students. In her chemistry course, she has more than one level in the class at the same time. In each class, she has chemistry students and honors chemistry students. Typically, her honors students move at a faster pace through the content and are ready for labs earlier than some of her other students. One way she differentiates for her honors students is to allow them to make a pre-lab video for the other students after they have completed a lab. She has found this to be very effective and motivating, both for her honors students and for those students who watch the pre-lab video later.

Record Student Experiments and Share with All Students

Enoch Ng is a fifth grade science and math teacher in Singapore. He has 38 kids in a class and still is able to do labs. One thing he often does is have students conduct different experiments along the same theme and creates video summaries from each group. For example, his class was investigating factors that affect the rate of evaporation of water. Some groups explored heat, others wind, others surface area, and others the amount of dissolved particles. Students conducted different experiments to test these effects in small groups, and when they finished, Ng filmed quick summaries of each experiment for different factors. He then edited these summaries into one video and required students to watch the summary video. Although he did not have time or the resources for all students to do all of the experiments, students were required to know all of the factors that affected evaporation. This video was the key to making this requirement possible. Ng makes sure students explain not just what they did, but more importantly, how what they did led them to their conclusions. This is an excellent way to help students to think scientifically as they explain natural phenomena.

Have Students Record Their Experiments

Marc Seigel, a chemistry teacher in New Jersey, has his students document their own experiments on video. Not only does he have them film their processes in the lab, but he also requires the students to probe deeper into the topic. Students analyze the data, derive conclusions, and include their conclusions in the video. Seigel found that when students film themselves, the activity brings out their deeper thinking. He thinks it has to do with the public nature of the videos, as all students in his class will see the final products.

FIGURE 4.2 Student records a video of her experiment using a smartphone.

Chapter 5

traditional resources and choice in flipped learning

ONE OF THE MISCONCEPTIONS about the flipped class is that it is just learning through video. It can appear that a flipped classroom is all about watching videos before class and then doing other things during class time. Though most teachers start with this, they quickly realize that the real benefit of flipping the classroom is reinventing the class time. What happens during class time is far more important than video creation and consumption.

Information clearly can be transferred using methods other than video. Students can read textbooks, read something online, learn through the inquiry process, learn by doing, and learn in numerous other ways. This chapter explores tools that complement instructional video and that can help teachers get away from lecture as the primary means of disseminating information. We also present the idea that giving students a choice can increase their engagement.

Some teachers have noted that they have been flipping their class for a long time—decades, in fact. They send students home to read a textbook and expect them to come to class prepared to engage in higher-order thinking. Pre-teaching models have been around for well over two centuries (Thayer Method, inverted classroom, etc.) So are these methods flipping? We encourage educators to avoid semantic arguments about whether something is flipped or not and focus on whether the needs of students are being met. Pedagogically, there is little difference between assigning a text to read, an activity to complete, a PowerPoint to click through, or a video to view. All of these methods are designed around the expectation that students will come to class prepared. Flipping the class with video is simply a way to reach a video-saturated culture in a familiar medium.

Textbooks

Most schools still issue students textbooks at the beginning of the year. Though many of these textbooks are now digital, they are textbooks nonetheless. We are not against textbooks. We see them as a valuable resource to help students learn. Flipped videos should not take the place of reading as a rule. However, be strategic about any textbook readings you assign. Keep assigning readings where appropriate and use flipped videos where appropriate.

Other Readings

Clearly, textbooks should not be the only reading resource we provide for students to interact with. We want students to read other text relating to science. Students can get information by reading scientific studies online, magazines dedicated to science, popular press items that feature new scientific discoveries, and, of course, science journals. Because some of these articles may contain inaccessible vocabulary or concepts, students may need to read the more complex content in class. In this case, students need an expert interpreter to help them access the content in these higher-level articles.

The Ideal Flipped Class: Choice

When we were traditional teachers, we simply taught our lessons to the whole group on our timetable. Students then went home and did homework. They got their information by attending class. Then we started flipping our classrooms, and students received information through video. For many reasons, this was better than the previous system, but there was still only *one* way to get information.

As we moved into our third year of flipping our class, we realized that not all students learn best from any one method (lecture or video). As a result, we realized that teaching through multiple modalities is the best way to organize a flipped classroom. We began to give students choices on how they want to learn new content. Some chose to learn by reading the textbook, others liked learning through videos, and still others needed hands-on activities to learn. Instead of simply assigning one reading, or one video, or one online simulation, we suggest you offer students a variety of options.

One particular student approached Jon and asked if he could skip the flipped videos. He asked if he could just read the textbook instead. The answer was clearly yes! If a student can learn better by reading a textbook, then there is no need for teachers to require them to view a video. If students learn better by reading, let them read; if they learn more effectively through online simulations, let them simulate. This may seem a bit chaotic and disorganized, but students naturally consume information in different ways, and ultimately, giving students a choice will help them all be more engaged in the learning process.

One way to implement choice into your flipped class is to create a choice board (Figure 5.1). The boards are set up so that students cannot simply complete the easy activities and avoid the hard ones. Instead, choice boards are set up so that students must do one knowledge-level activity, followed by an application-level activity, followed by an analysis-level activity. The choice board approach uses Bloom's taxonomy as a basis for determining levels of cognition.

Developing choice boards and the corresponding activities will take a considerable amount of time. We do not recommend that teachers who are new to the flipped class start with choice boards. Developing a library of videos and getting quality activities in class will need to be the first priority, but as a teacher moves along, choice boards could be a powerful addition to their class.

	Knowledge/ Understanding- Level Activities	Application- Level Activities	Higher Order/ Hands-On Activities
Activity 1	Read textbook and take notes.	Worksheet (Odd questions)	Experiment A
Activity 2	Watch video, take notes, and interact with the video using online tools.	Worksheet (Even questions)	Experiment B
Activity 3	Search the learning objective online and summarize your findings.	Interactive Online Simulation Meet with your teacher and explain the concepts.	Student Project Design your own experiment that demonstrates the key point of this objective.

FIGURE 5.1 This example choice board gives students the freedom to choose the activity that most appeals to them.

One of the most commonly asked questions about a flipped classroom is, "If I'm not lecturing any more, what am I supposed to do during class?" In the next chapter, we offer some specific examples of how to reinvent your class time.

Chapter 6

rethinking class time

BECAUSE A FLIPPED classroom frees up more time with students, the most important question to answer is what to do with the recovered class time. Ultimately, there is no "right" answer to that question, but it is imperative that teachers begin the process of rethinking how to use the face-to-face time in class with students together as a group. This chapter focuses on some ways in which you can maximize class time to help students move to deeper levels of understanding and truly learn science.

Individualized Instruction

We can summarize all of the strategies in this chapter with the term "individualized instruction." Under a more traditional model of instruction, students receive instruction according to the pre-established pace of the class. In a flipped classroom, students get assistance with content right when they need it.

Guided Practice

In a flipped class, students have more time for guided practice. As chemistry teachers, we used to send our students home to work on problems, write up lab reports, and in general conduct higher-order cognitive tasks. However, many students went home and struggled. For whatever reason, they missed crucial content in class and simply couldn't do the homework. Students then came to class frustrated with incomplete work and deeply rooted misconceptions. Simply flipping your class gives students time to work on problems with the teacher present. This is revolutionary for learning because teachers can spend considerably more time circulating around the classroom assisting students. This individualized instructional assistance time may be the single greatest benefit to a flipped classroom. Students who struggle get the help they need. With the increased student-teacher time, there is simply more time to assist struggling students—and there is also more time to challenge the high-achieving students who are ready for more.

Small-Group Tutorials

During guided practice, teachers often have several students who struggle with similar content. Recovered class time allows teachers to engage them in small groups to review difficult concepts or clear up jointly held misconceptions.

For example, while circulating around his classroom, Jon discovered a number of students with incorrect ideas about gravity. He formed a small group and spent time correcting their misconceptions.

Students may also struggle with problems such as how to balance an equation or how to calculate the normal force. In such cases, we recommend that you bring those students together for a mini-tutorial at the whiteboard and direct them to solve the problems. Teachers can also take students to a digital whiteboard and record the mini help sessions. The students in the small group now have access to a video record of the discussion to review later. In our experience, students found this level of personalization very helpful because they had a tutorial video made just for them, which covered the difficult concepts with which *they* were struggling. These help sessions also became available to other students to access in case they needed assistance with the same topic.

Peer Tutoring

Although there is value in students wrestling with content on their own, it is amazing to observe students helping each other learn. Students who have just learned something can often be better teachers than we are because the learning process is so fresh in their minds. A novice who has just learned something new can provide meaningful insight to his or her peers about learning the same concept. This creates a collaborative atmosphere where students work together to comprehend a new concept. It also builds a sense of community. In many ways, this mirrors the ad hoc study groups many of us organized in college, but it now happens in K–12 classrooms, with the added benefit that the teacher is present to help the group when it reaches an impasse.

Science Demonstrations

One of our favorite things to do in science classes was demonstrations. As chemistry teachers, we had no lack of demonstrations we could do for our students. We regularly used to set things on fire and show discrepant events we wanted students to understand. In a flipped class, you can take these demonstrations to the next level.

One common question science teachers have about flipped learning is whether they should conduct demonstrations in class or on a video. Our recommendation is doing as many live demos in class as possible. They are amazing learning opportunities that students need to experience for themselves. They need to feel the heat of the exploding methane balloon, they need to touch the bones of a skeleton, they need to see the falling monkey get hit by the projectile.

There are some demos you might want to present on a video, however. One example could be monitoring the temperature of ice to water to steam. This particular demo involves the long task of boiling water, which is about as exciting as, well, watching water boil. If you did this demo on a video, you could spare your students the 20 minutes it typically takes to heat the water from zero to 100 Celsius. Demos, along with anything else, still come down to the one question: What is the best use of your face-to-face time with your students? If the best use of that time is to watch water boil (along with the other educational benefits of monitoring the heating curve of water), then do that. But if there is a better and more efficient way to have students experience something, then modify the presentation to make better use of your students' time. Use flipped videos to help maximize your class time so you can do all the great demos science teachers love to do.

Peer Instruction

Teachers all over the globe use the peer instruction teaching method to engage students during class time. Eric Mazur, a physics professor at Harvard University, developed peer instruction in 1991. He was dissatisfied with students' conceptual learning in his traditional lecture classes and looked for a way to reinvigorate his class and help students develop deeper understandings of key physics content. Peer instruction, which is often paired with just-in-time teaching for out-of-class work, is backed by 20 years of research that demonstrates increased learning outcomes, including problem-solving skills, conceptual understanding, and decreasing the gender gap in the sciences (Schell, Lukoff, & Mazur, 2013). Studies conducted by math teacher Troy Faulkner in the high school mathematics context at Byron High School in Byron, Minnesota, also demonstrate that when peer instruction is used in conjunction with flipped learning, student achievement is increased (Fulton, 2012).

Peer instruction has seven nonnegotiable steps. We adapted the following from Julie Schell's blog post at http://blog.peerinstruction.net/2012/07/03/choreography-of-a-flipped-classroom.

1. Assign a "coverage" task — a reading, video, or activity — or provide a mini-lecture on a particular concept. These are videos that students would typically watch before class in a flipped classroom. For example, have students watch this video on gravity at bit.ly/flipgravity.

2. Begin a round of questioning (Round 1): Pose a question related to the coverage activity to students and solicit individual responses. Students must commit to one answer. You can collect responses with low-tech tools such as cards, or higher-tech tools such as a student response

system. With our example video mentioned earlier, the following question is appropriate:

If the Moon were twice the distance from the Earth as it is today, how much would the force of gravity change between the Earth and the Moon?

a) It would not be any different

b) It would be twice as weak

c) It would be four times as weak

d) It would be less, but you cannot determine how much less

e) It would be higher

f) None of the above

The video does not directly answer this example question. The question is an application of the concepts found in the video. The key in developing good peer instruction questions is to develop questions that allow students to apply conceptual understanding. These are typically at higher-order levels of cognition (think Applying or above on Bloom's taxonomy).

3. Teachers analyze student responses.

4. Group students based on response.

5. Put students into groups of between two and four students in which not all of the students have chosen the same answer. Cue them to find someone with a different answer and try to defend their answers with reasoning. During this conversation, students try to understand the question together.

6. Begin round 2 of questioning. Re-poll the students. You should expect to see a shift to the right answer after discussion.

7. Discuss any misconceptions. Not all students will get the answer correct, so a class discussion about the question at hand is worth the conversation.

If you would like to read more about this method, we recommend Mazur's book *Peer Instruction* (Mazur, 1997). He spends the first six chapters discussing the model, and then the rest of the book is about specific physics activities you can do with your students. If you are looking for non-physics examples, we suggest you search the internet for "ConcepTests." You will find chemistry, biology, and Earth science peer instruction activities.

Now that you have flipped your class, you can take it even further by using the flipped-mastery approach. The next chapter explains how a flipped science class can transition to an asynchronous mastery learning environment where students must demonstrate mastery of objectives before moving on.

Chapter 7

mastery learning
in the
flipped classroom

ALTHOUGH WE ADDRESSED the approach we call flipped-mastery in detail in our first book, here we dig a bit deeper into the topic as it pertains to science education. Mastery learning is not a new development in education; it was developed in the middle of the 20th century by Benjamin Bloom of Bloom's taxonomy fame. Essentially, mastery learning is a system in which learners must demonstrate understanding, or "mastery," of a particular topic before moving through the rest of the course material. Mastery learning works especially well for subjects that are linear in sequence and build off material learned earlier in the course. Learn A before learning B before learning C, because you will not understand C without understanding B, and you will not understand B without understanding A. Mathematically based sciences, math, grammar, and mechanics of language are subjects that lend themselves nicely to this approach.

In a flipped-mastery setting, students work through the course material at their own pace by accessing instructional video content, problem sets, labs, demonstrations, and other learning objects when they are ready for them. Operating in an asynchronous environment like this allows students the flexibility to learn at a pace that is appropriate for them. It has an added advantage in that it can solve issues of access for students without sufficient technology at home. In a flipped-mastery classroom, video content can easily be accessed in class. Flipped-mastery is often the second iteration of a flipped classroom that builds off the video library a teacher has developed through the first phase of flipping his or her class.

Flipped-mastery places more control of learning into the hands of the students because it allows them the flexibility to create their own schedules of learning based around their own learning needs and styles. Some students may need some additional support and structure in a mastery environment, and providing students with daily, weekly, or monthly goals is one way to help them avoid getting behind. This system also allows high-achieving students to move more quickly through the course material and gives them time to work on independent projects of their own design.

Demonstrations in Flipped-Mastery

One of the most exciting aspects of teaching science is conducting demonstrations in class. Because of the asynchronous nature of a flipped-mastery classroom, the dynamics of in-class demonstrations will change because students will no longer gather as a whole class to observe. Demos in a flipped-mastery class are conducted asynchronously, where a teacher conducts the demonstration multiple times when students are ready for it. The benefit of this approach is that instead of students straining to see from the back of a class, the demos are conducted with four or five students in a closer, more intimate setting that allows all students to see and ask questions. Given that many demos consist of discrepant events that generate many questions in the minds of students, conducting demos in this more intimate setting allows more students to raise questions and have them answered and discussed by the teacher.

The challenge, however, is that demos are often done as demos, rather than labs, because of the cost associated with the materials or the difficulty of setting up the demonstration. In cases like this, use professional judgment to determine if a whole-class demonstration might be appropriate. You don't want to pick up liquid nitrogen every morning for a month on your way to school. Cases like that may require you to call an all-stop with the class and gather everyone, ready or not, to see an exciting demonstration. Not all students may be academically prepared for the content of the demo, but they will no doubt enjoy it nonetheless.

Labs in Flipped-Mastery

Labs in a flipped-mastery classroom can be a challenge to manage because different students will need them every day, and the materials may need to be left set up for many days or weeks at time. We recommend setting up small stations for each lab containing the appropriate materials for the students to use. Although this might seem a bit chaotic and unsafe, the teacher has the added benefit of giving a safety briefing to a small group of students rather than to the class as a whole. As with the demos, you may need to have the entire class conduct some labs on one day. Live specimens have a life span, some reagents have a shelf life, and teachers should not leave 12 M HCl out around the classroom for days on end.

Some teachers flip the lab instructions and safety briefings by creating an instructional video, linking it to a QR code, and then pasting the QR code above the lab station. For those unfamiliar with QR codes, these are similar to bar codes on products at a store. QR codes are scannable links to online resources using free online QR code generators. Mobile apps are available to scan the QR code, taking the user to the appropriately linked online resource.

When a group of students is ready to conduct a lab with a QR code, they scan it with a mobile device and have a specific lab video load to their device for immediate viewing. In addition, a flipped-mastery lab will help cut costs by eliminating the need for class sets of equipment, because only a few groups will be conducting the lab at any given time. Consider raising this when discussing the flipped model with your administration.

Making the Jump to Flipped-Mastery

Jumping into flipped-mastery is a big step. Many teachers flip their class and never move to flipped-mastery. We say emphatically that the move we made from Flipped Class 101 to flipped-mastery was the best thing we ever did in our careers. It was hard, but the level of learning and the degree to which our students took ownership of their learning was proof to us that this step was the right decision.

To learn more about how to implement the flipped-mastery model, we encourage you to read the second half of our first book, *Flip Your Classroom*, and read *Flipped Learning*, which has some teachers discussing how they moved to flipped-mastery.

Some science teachers have gravitated toward the flipped-mastery approach, but others are trying to find a way to merge flipped learning with an inquiry-based approach to learning science. The next chapter explains how inquiry and flipping can complement each other.

Chapter 8

inquiry
and
flipped learning

MANY SCIENCE TEACHERS have taken the flipped learning model and adapted it to operate in conjunction with or alongside various other science teaching and learning strategies, including guided inquiry and POGIL, modeling, and lab-driven learning. Some have suggested that flipped learning is incompatible with more constructivist approaches to learning. However, given that flipped learning is a flexible and adaptable model, we feel these claims are unwarranted.

Process Oriented Guided Inquiry Learning (POGIL)

Bruce Wellman, a science and engineering teacher, author, and trainer, has successfully merged flipped learning with certain elements of his Process Oriented Guided Inquiry Learning (POGIL) classroom. One of the reasons Wellman is so passionate about POGIL is because of how it helps his students develop their own cognitive framework, and how it increases students' ability to develop a scientific argument from various forms of evidence. However, he is also very concerned with the efficiency of any teaching method he employs.

Although POGIL has proven to be an effective way to teach (Moog, Creegan, Hanson, Spencer, & Straumanis, 2006) it is not always the most efficient. For example, a POGIL exercise exists to teach students how to read a graduated cylinder. But the time it takes to go through the activity is not always the most efficient use of class time. A short video tutorial can accomplish the same learning outcome in much less time, freeing up class time to apply what was learned about using a graduated cylinder.

What remains to be seen is whether a POGIL activity or a flipped video is more effective in long-term retention of the skill. Wellman believes that short instructional videos are most effective for basic techniques and skills, such as using lab equipment, reading instruments, performing stoichiometric calculations, and other procedural and repeatable skills. In addition, there are particular topics that lend themselves more to POGIL. These include abstract concepts such as intermolecular forces, solubility phenomena, and bonding, which are more suited to a guided inquiry approach than is a more algorithmic skill like stoichiometric calculations.

Explore-Flip-Apply

So far we have explored how POGIL can be used to better teach one topic, while flipped learning can be used to teach other topics. Can inquiry and flipped learning be used in conjunction with one another to teach one particular topic?

The inquiry process is predicated on the idea that students need to investigate something on their own and go through the process of concept development without receiving prior instruction. Beginning with an instructional video would not be compatible with a true inquiry approach because front-loading the inquiry process will rob students of the opportunity to explore concepts on their own. However, as any teacher who has used inquiry-based learning knows, not every student comes away from the experience with an accurate or comprehensive understanding of the learning target. The process students undertake to arrive at their conclusions is often beneficial, but students may have learned inaccurate information or come to invalid conclusions along the way.

This does not invalidate the inquiry process, but it does expose an opportunity for the teacher to intervene with direct instruction. It also allows the teacher to intervene only with the individuals who actually need intervention. Instead of spraying the entire class with content, the teacher directs the students who have reached poor conclusions or are developing misconceptions to appropriate content. In this model, a flipped video would be used in the middle of the inquiry process to help clarify and solidify what students have already learned through the inquiry process.

This idea of using video as an intervention in the middle of an inquiry process is what Ramsey Musallam calls Explore-Flip-Apply: engage the students in inquiry, intervene with video (for those students who have reached invalid conclusions), then have students apply what they have learned (www.cyclesoflearning.com/learning--instruction/explore-flip-apply-example).

Modeling

One science teaching and learning technique that may, at first glance, appear to be incompatible with flipped learning is modeling. Modeling is an inquiry approach to learning, but is somewhat less guided and less structured than POGIL. Students undergo inquiry processes together as a class, share their results on whiteboards, and develop viable conceptual and mathematical models based on what was uncovered through the data they collected. Modeling is rooted in constructivist learning theory and, in its pure form, does not allow any direct instruction. According to physics teacher and modeling proponent Mark Hughes, there are very few modeling purists out there who couldn't find some benefit from flipped techniques. Hughes says, "Modeling is based on Socratic dialogue, which is an effective, though not always efficient, way of teaching through the process of questioning. However, some Modeling proponents are so inflexible with their techniques that the Socratic dialogue can become the Socratic Inquisition." This has not dissuaded Mark from continuing the use of modeling in his class, but he approaches the technique flexibly. He records the whiteboarding sessions for students who miss class. Absent students receive an experience that is not the modeling experience, but it is better than no learning experience at all. He also realizes that students in the modeling classroom must learn and master certain necessary skills to be successful modelers. Skills such as graphing and determining the equation of a line can efficiently be taught through direct instruction so the students can use them in the modeling process.

Hughes, like Wellman, agrees that repeatable skills and techniques are great applications for flipped learning, whereas deeper concepts and more abstract ideas are better taught through inquiry. Both teachers approach their educational ideals as realists. Both teach real kids with real struggles and, in Hughes's case, 40 at a time in each class period. Both teachers have found that flipped learning can help them be more efficient educators— a necessary thing in our current educational climate, where teachers are responsible for students learning specific curricula and are often held accountable for student performance on a variety of standardized tests. There are times when ideology must be modified to meet the needs of students.

Flipped learning is compatible with modified applications of both POGIL and modeling, but has limited overlap with a pure application of either. Both POGIL and modeling are examples of lab-based instructional techniques in which labs are used, not to reinforce what has already been learned, but rather to engage the learner as the primary tool for learning. However, to learn through lab and inquiry, certain skills and techniques are necessary. One challenge that a science teacher faces is that all students bring different skill levels and technique mastery with them. All students are required to abide by certain safety procedures, all students need to know how to graph, and all students need to know how to use basic lab equipment. Some students will come to class with these abilities from prior coursework, and others will come to class with no skills whatsoever. Using flipped learning to teach these skills and techniques allows those who already understand them to proceed without being held back, and it allows those who need to develop these skills the flexibility to do so without affecting the progress of the class as a whole.

Interactive Simulations

There are a host of online simulations that can take the place of direct instruction for students. These simulations are ideally used as simple inquiry activities that are easy to implement. They engage students with natural phenomena that are difficult to reproduce and measure in a typical school laboratory or classroom.

Students interact with virtual objects that correspond with reality. These simulations allow students to explore key concepts by changing variables and discovering for themselves what would occur. Such simulations are useful and can take the place of direct instruction though flipped videos. Students can learn more deeply via this discovery approach than through interacting with videos on the same topic. And learning through these simulations can be faster than some inquiry labs because of how efficiently students can manipulate variables in a virtual environment.

Following are some examples of online simulations:

- PHET Interactive Simulations (http://phet. colorado.edu) is a free resource made by a team at the University of Colorado.

- Explore Learning Gizmos (www.explorelearning. com) is a subscription service with math and science simulations.

- The Molecular Workbench (http://workbench. concord.org/database) is a list of interactive science simulations in ecology, physics, and chemistry.

Many textbooks also include simulations that tie directly into the textbook content that teachers may already be teaching.

Simulations are ideal, though not necessary, for teachers who have access to an interactive whiteboard. Small groups of students can gather around the interactive board and collaboratively experience these simulations together. Many of these simulations also have guided activities that may be valuable in helping students make sense of the content.

Transitioning to project-based learning (PBL) is natural in a flipped classroom. The next chapter explains how flipped videos can support PBL.

Chapter 9

project-based learning and genius hour

MANY TEACHERS THINK they are doing PBL because they have their students do projects. In reality, however, PBL is much more than projects. According to the Buck Institute for Education, PBL is a teaching method where students gain knowledge and skills by working for an extended period to investigate and respond to a complex question, problem, or challenge (definition taken from http://bie.org/about/what_pbl).

PBL in the Science Classroom

The Buck Institute has been studying the efficacy of PBL for many years. They have shown PBL to be an effective way to teach standards and content without the use of direct instruction. Many teachers using flipped learning have found that the extra time they gain allows them the flexibility to explore strategies like PBL while still maintaining a library of content that is delivered regularly or as needed. Science teachers in particular are excited about PBL because so many science, technology, engineering, and mathematics (STEM) projects are available for students.

Science is a natural fit for PBL, and flipped learning is proving to be a gateway for science teachers to give it a try. Even if a teacher does not teach a content-heavy subject that requires a great deal of content delivery, flipped videos can be used in project-oriented courses such as robotics or engineering to teach background information or essential skills. Rather than teaching an entire class how to perform a particular task, make a tutorial that students can access when they are ready to learn. Wellman does exactly this. He uses video content in his engineering courses to train his students on basic skills. He has found that his students come to him with such a wide variety of skills and backgrounds that making use of video as an asynchronous teaching tool is one of the only ways he can meet the individual learning needs of his students.

Robotics and engineering teacher Erin Hopkins runs an entirely project-based class. Her students prepare for competitions by designing, testing, and modifying robots. However, she has found that some of her students learn at different paces, especially when using drafting software. Some of her students are familiar with the software when they arrive, and others have no experience with it. Some of her students pick up the skills quickly; others need more time. To accommodate everyone, Hopkins uses instructional videos to teach the software rather than teaching the class as a whole. This allows all students to move through the content at their own pace, and it allows them to work on drafting projects that are in alignment with their current skill level. Given that all students view content while in class, some may hesitate to call this flipped learning. However, the term "in-flip" is often used to describe this use of asynchronous instruction in which all the work is done in class. The power of flipped learning goes beyond using video as homework. The power lies in the delivery of instruction to individual learners.

Genius Hour or 20% Time

Dan Pink's book *Drive* (Pink, 2009) has led some flipped classroom teachers to use the time they recover by flipping to implement Genius Hour or 20% time. *Drive* is about what motivates people to do what they do, and how to help motivate people in an ethical and natural way. The ideas stem from companies like 3M and Google, who give their employees 20% of their work time to passionately focus on unassigned projects. In the classroom, 20% time generally allows students one day per week to work on noncurricular projects that are related in some way to the subject of study. Katie Lanier, a physics teacher in Allen, Texas, decided that although flipping her class gave her more time in class, she would give that recovered time back to the students. Lanier has implemented 20% time to allow students the opportunity to explore the physical world on their own, and they have developed custom-built quadcopters, designed energy-efficient structures, and mastered the art of working collaboratively on projects. She could have used the time for more instruction, more labs, or more practice, but she decided to let the students explore on their own and develop as scientists and engineers.

Chapter 10

conclusion

SOME EDUCATORS have asked us to provide a step-by-step guide to flipping their classrooms. Although this book serves to provide specific guidelines to science teachers, these should be just that—guidelines. There is no one way to flip your class. Nor should there be. The flipped class needs to be customized and contextualized for each teacher's class, for their school population, and for each teacher's personal style. The worst mistake you could make is to try to replicate everything in this book to flip your class. Instead, we want you to use this as a guide from which you will adopt practices that make the most sense in your context.

We had one goal in writing this—to move teachers away from the front of the room and to encourage teachers to create active learning environments where *all students* are engaged in their own learning. A recent white paper entitled "Teaching for Rigor: A Call for a Critical Instructional Shift" from the Marzano Research Group discussed what instructional strategies educators are actually using in classrooms. Marzano (Marzano & Toth, 2014) and his group, which collected more than 2 million data points from the United States, found that:

- 58% of all classroom time is being used for interacting with new content. The majority of this time is dedicated to direct instruction.

- 36% of classroom time is used for practicing and deepening content.

- 6% of classroom time is used for cognitively complex tasks involving generating and testing hypotheses.

These numbers need to change, especially in the classrooms of science teachers. Science doesn't happen in textbooks. To quote Ms. Frizzle from the children's television program *The Magic School Bus*, we must "Take chances, make mistakes, and get messy."

In case you feel we are unrealistic about the real world in which there are state tests, end-of-course exams, and high expectations, know that we still believe there is a place for direct instruction and content delivery. Students often don't know what they don't know, and we science teachers can help them through that discernment process. We have much to teach our students, but the reality is that many of us wishfully desire to do more inquiry, more labs, more differentiation, and more projects. Yet the tyranny of curriculum and the comfort of our old ways often keep us in a rut. We are seeing around the world that the flipped class is proving to be a way for science teachers to move toward more active forms of learning.

Take, for example, Jasper Fox, Jr., a middle school Earth science teacher in New York. Like many of us, he was stuck in the rut of direct instruction with an occasional lab thrown in for good measure. He eventually embraced the flipped classroom model, and as he did, his class was transformed from a place for information transfer into a center of learning. He first flipped his class using the Flipped Class 101 model, but soon realized he could do more. His next step was to implement mastery learning into his classroom. So he implemented the flipped-mastery model, and then realized that there was even more that he could do. His next step was to incorporate modeling and standards-based grading into his class. Jasper has adopted all of these techniques in an attempt to move away from a vocabulary-driven form of instruction to one of inquiry, exploration, and making.

Although Jasper believes strongly in inquiry, he recognizes that most students lack certain prerequisite skills to engage in pure inquiry. "Most students," Jasper said, "are not where Leonardo da Vinci was when he invented and discovered most of his work. Da Vinci needed some background learning before he became an explorer of the world, and my students need some scaffolding to help them become capable of pure inquiry." He has used flipped learning to help free up time for his students to engage in more interesting and meaningful learning in class. By taking the best of all these models, and not trying to apply any of them in their "pure" forms, he has developed an atmosphere of inquiry and exploration while still ensuring his students are exposed to the required content for his courses. As a result, Jasper has found a way to secure high performance by his students on state exams while allowing students to learn in a non-oppressive, inquiry-driven environment in which learning, rather than acquisition of points, is the goal.

Jasper has customized and contextualized the flipped learning model for *his* situation, *his* style of teaching, and *his* students. In that spirit we encourage you use this book as a guide. Do not consider it a set of rules that you must follow. Our challenge to you is to do what Jasper has done. Find the parts of the flipped classroom model that work for you and merge it with the good teaching practices you have been doing for years or wish you could be doing.

We encourage you to take these action steps to get started:

- **Take an honest look.** What percentage of your class time is involved in direct instruction or practice? Before we flipped our classes, our numbers were similar to the data from the Marzano Research Group, and you may be in a similar situation. Think carefully about how flipping your class could help your students spend less time with new content and more time working on more challenging cognitive tasks.

- **Choose to begin.** Flip at least one lesson, or start by recording your live lessons for one year. What one lesson or topic do students in your class typically struggle with, so that you find yourself repeating it over and over? That is the perfect lesson to be your first flip.

- **Communicate.** The flipped classroom may be a new concept for students, parents, and administrators. Before you flip, develop an action plan to share reasons why you are flipping your class and to communicate your expectations to all stakeholders, including students, parents, and administrators.

- **Plan your flip.** It can be difficult to jump right into a fully flipped class. It may be better for you to look carefully at your existing course materials and spend some time planning how each lesson might (or might not) be adapted to accommodate video as an instructional tool.

- **Learn more.** This book is an introduction for science teachers. Pick up a copy of *Flip Your Classroom* and the accompanying workbook. If you are at all intrigued with the flipped-mastery model, the second half of *Flip Your Classroom* focuses on how to implement it.

The world of information has dramatically changed since most of us were in school. We grew up in an information-scarce world where information "lived" in libraries, books, and the heads of our teachers. Today we live in a saturated world where information is easily accessible to anyone with an internet-ready device. Whatever you teach, whether it is middle school life science, Earth science, chemistry, biology, or AP Physics, there is now an instructional video on YouTube that teaches everything in your curriculum. There are countless videos on Newton's first law, on how to balance an oxidation-reduction reaction, on the causes of earthquakes, on mitosis, and so on.

If a YouTube video can replace us, we should be replaced! We realize this is a strong statement, but hear us out. Teachers are no longer the keepers of information, so our roles must change. We need to move away from being disseminators of content and instead become facilitators of learning. As we embrace our new roles, we will be adding more value to our students' learning experiences. Instead of being replaced by a computer or a video, we are becoming more necessary and integral to education—because only teachers can help students explore topics more deeply, and only a content-area and learning expert can diagnose where students struggle. In a flipped classroom, the teacher is actually more necessary, more needed, and more integral to the learning experience of all students. We are adding value beyond the content. We are ushering our students into an environment in which they take ownership of their learning.

Will you embrace the flipped classroom? Will you take on the challenge of changing your practice?

references

Bergmann, J., & Sams, A. (2012). *Flip your classroom: Reach every student in every class every day.* Eugene, OR: ISTE/ASCD.

Bergmann, J., & Sams, A. (2014). *Flipped learning: Gateway to student engagement.* Eugene, OR: ISTE.

Bloom, B. S. (1968). Learning for mastery. *UCLA-CSEIP Evaluation Comment, 2,* 1–12.

Fulton, K. (2012). Upside down and inside out: Flip your classroom to improve student learning. *Learning & Leading with Technology,* June/July, 12–17.

Marzano, R., & Toth, M. (2014, March). *Teaching for rigor.* Rep. Marzano Research Labs. Retrieved from www.marzanocenter.com/essentials/teaching-for-rigor-landing

Mazur, E. (1997). *Peer instruction: A user's manual.* Upper Saddle River, NJ: Prentice Hall.

Moog, R. S., Creegan, F. J., Hanson, D. M., Spencer, J. N., & Straumanis, A. R. (2006). Process-oriented guided inquiry learning: POGIL and the POGIL Project. *Metropolitan Universities Journal, 17,* 41–51.

Pink, D. H. (2009). *Drive: The surprising truth about what motivates us*. New York, NY: Riverhead Books.

Schell, J., Lukoff, B., & Mazur, E. (2013). Catalyzing learner engagement using cutting-edge classroom response systems in higher education. In C. Wankel & P. Blessinger (Eds.), *Increasing student engagement and retention using classroom technologies: Classroom response systems and mediated discourse technologies* (pp. 233–261). Bingley, England: Emerald Publishing Group.